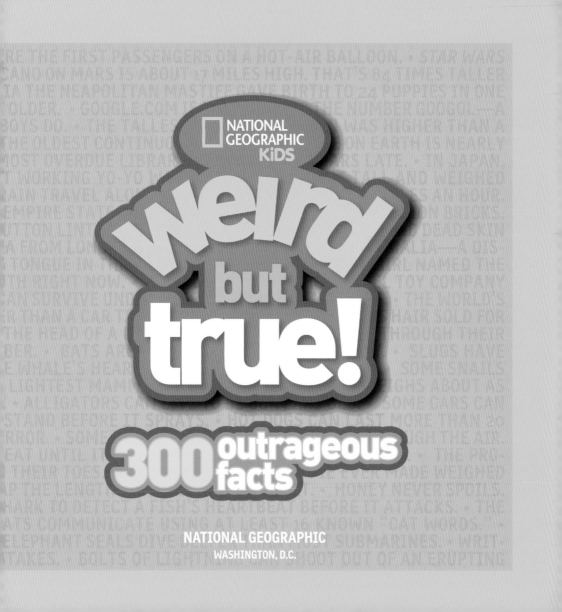

NATIONAL GEOGRAPHIC
KiDS

weird but true!

300 outrageous facts

NATIONAL GEOGRAPHIC
WASHINGTON, D.C.

Cheetahs can change direction in midair when **chasing prey.**

A SHEEP, A DUCK, AND A ROOSTER WERE THE FIRST PASSENGERS ON A HOT-AIR BALLOON.

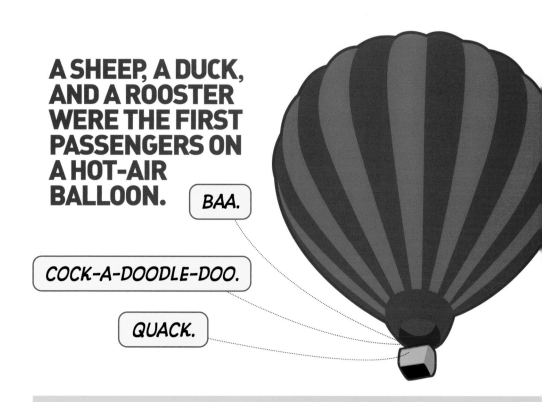

BAA.

COCK-A-DOODLE-DOO.

QUACK.

Google.com is named after the number googol—

10000000000000000000
00000000000000000000
00000000000000000000

Tia the **Neapolitan mastiff** gave birth to **24 puppies** in one litter.

Girls have more taste buds than **boys** do.

ne followed by a hundred zeros.

OOOOOOOOOOOOOOOOO
OOOOOOOOOOOOOOOOO
OOOOOOOOOOOOOOOOO

The tallest known snowman was higher than a 12-story building.

SOME HONEYBEE QUEENS QUACK.

A bat can eat 3,000 **insects** in one **night.**

The most overdue library book was 288 years late.

The **largest working yo-yo** was more than 10 feet (3 m) tall and weighed almost 900 pounds (408 kg) —as much as a **polar bear.**

***Star Wars* creators designed Yoda to look like Albert Einstein.**

IN JAPAN, IT'S POSSIBLE TO BUY WATERMELONS SHAPED LIKE PYRAMIDS.

167 letters

Krungthe
Ratanakosin Mahintha
Mahadilokpop Nopa
Udomratchanivet Mah
Avatarnsathit Sakkat
officially known a

re in the world's longest
lace-name,

ahanakhon Bovorn
yutthaya
cratchathani Burirom
than Amornpiman
ctiyavisnukarmprasit,
angkok, Thailand.

New York City's Empire State Building was built with ten million bricks.

A coffin was once designed to look like a lobster.

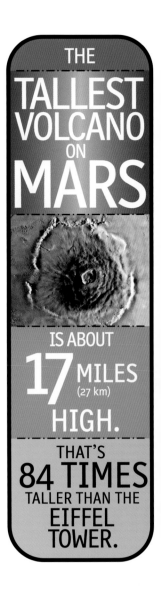

THE **TALLEST VOLCANO ON MARS**

IS ABOUT **17** MILES (27 km) **HIGH.**

THAT'S **84 TIMES** TALLER THAN THE **EIFFEL TOWER.**

PEANUT BUTTER CAN BE CONVERTED INTO A DIAMOND.

If you could travel the speed of light, you would never get older.

BELLY BUTTON LINT

IS MADE OF CLOTHING FIBERS, HAIR, AND DEAD SKIN CELLS.

THE **OLDEST CONTINUOUSLY STANDING TREE** ON EARTH IS NEARLY 5,000 YEARS OLD— ABOUT THE SAME AGE AS THE PYRAMIDS OF **EGYPT.**

A woman hand-delivered a pizza

from **London, England, to Melbourne, Australia—** a distance of about **10,350 miles.**

(16,657 km)

Your **FINGERNAILS** take six months to grow from base to tip.

AN 11-YEAR-OLD **GIRL NAMED** THE DWARF PLANET **PLUTO.**

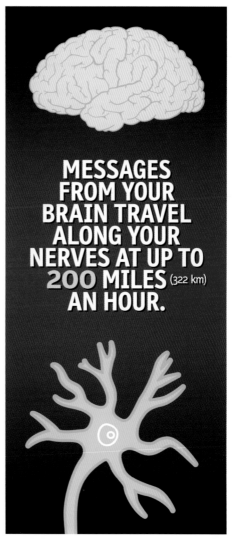

MESSAGES FROM YOUR BRAIN TRAVEL ALONG YOUR NERVES AT UP TO **200 MILES** (322 km) AN HOUR.

A SNEEZE TRAVELS 100 MILES AN HOUR.

(161 km)

A MAN KNOTTED 39 CHERRY STEMS WITH HIS TONGUE IN 3 MINUTES.

The world's **biggest flower**—found in the Indonesian rain forest—can grow **wider than a car tire.**

THE FOUNDERS OF T
TOY COMPAN
DOLLS AFTER THEI
KEN AND
BARB

MATTEL
NAMED TWO
CHILDREN:

E.

THERE ARE ABOUT A BILLION BACTERIA IN YOUR MOUTH RIGHT NOW.

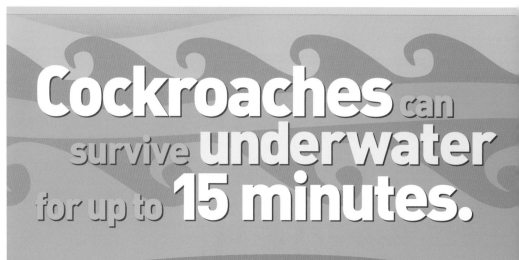

Cockroaches can survive underwater for up to 15 minutes.

The first bubble gum, made in 1906, was called Blibber-Blubber.

ABOUT **TEN** THOUSAND OF THE CELLS IN YOUR BODY COULD FIT ON THE HEAD OF A PIN.

Applesauce was the first food eaten in space by an American astronaut.

Phasmophobia is the fear of ghosts.

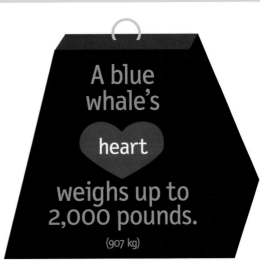

A blue whale's **heart** weighs up to 2,000 pounds. (907 kg)

Slugs have 3,000 teeth!

and 4 noses.

A
lock of
Elvis
Presley's
hair sold for
$115,120.

SOME CARS
CAN RUN ON
USED FRENCH-
FRY OIL.

HOT DOGS
CAN LAST MORE THAN 20 YEARS
IN LANDFILLS.

The eastern spotted **skunk** does *a handstand* before it **sprays.**

About a million Earths could fit inside the **sun.**

THE BRIGHTEST LIGHT ON A HOTEL—IN LAS VEGAS, NEVADA, IN THE UNITED STATES— CAN BE SEEN FROM AIRPLANES 250 MILES AWAY. (402 km)

THE PROTOTYPE OF THE ORIGINAL G.I. JOE DOLL SOLD FOR $200,000.

Almost **90%** of snow is air.

THE WORLD'S LIGHTEST MAMMAL
—THE BUMBLEBEE BAT—
WEIGHS ABOUT AS MUCH AS TWO M&M'S.

MOTHS CAN SMELL EACH OTHER FROM MILES AWAY.

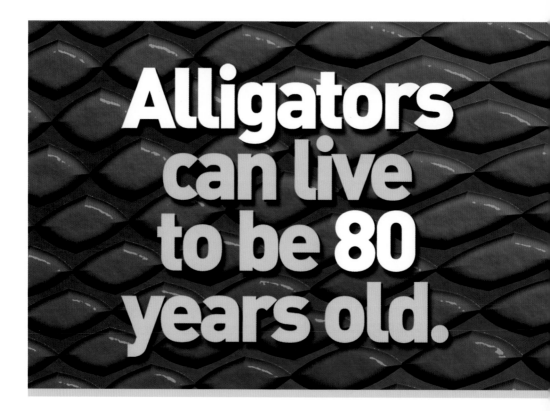

Alligators can live to be 80 years old.

A large python can swal

Bats

are the only
mammals
that fly.

SOME SNAILS CAN SLEEP
FOR THREE YEARS.

ow a goat whole.

SOME FROGS CAN GLIDE UP TO 50 FEET (15 m) THROUGH THE AIR.

A camel doesn't **sweat** until its body temperature reaches 106°F. (41°c)

Writers once used **bread crumbs** instead of **erasers** to correct pencil mistakes.

A waterfall in Hawaii sometimes goes up instead of down.

Cats communicate using at least 16 known "cat words."

A beefalo is part bison, part cow.

A man **sculpted a statue** of himself using his own **hair, teeth, and nails.**

IF GRASSHOPPERS WERE THE SIZE OF PEOPLE, THEY COULD LEAP THE LENGTH OF A BASKETBALL COURT.

BOLTS OF LIGHTNING CAN SHOOT OUT OF AN ERUPTING VOLCANO.

HORSES RUN ON THEIR toes.

Dragonflies can see in **all** directions at once.

There
are

29

different
shades of
red Crayola
crayons.

brick red

magenta

red

violet red

red violet

wild strawb...

IT'S POSSIBLE FOR A SHARK TO DETECT A **FISH'S HEARTBEAT** BEFORE IT ATTACKS.

You can buy a piece of meteorite on eBay.

THE **clock** ON THE **hundred-dollar bill** SAYS **4:10.**

WEDDING GOWNS HAVE BEEN MADE OUT OF TOILET PAPER

SOME FISH CAN WALK ON LAND.

You can see a **1,700-pound** (771 kg) chocolate moose named **Lenny** in Maine, in the U.S.A.

Scuba divers send postcards from a mailbox off the coast of **Japan** that's nearly **33 feet** (10 m) underwater.

The **LARGEST pumpkin pie WEIGHED 2,020 pounds** (916 kg).

DOLPHINS CAN HEAR SOUNDS UNDERWATER FROM 15 MILES (24 km) AWAY.

African elephants have ears shaped like the continent of **Africa.**

Porcupines CAN float.

An average yawn lasts about six seconds.

Koalas
and
humans
have similar
fingerprints.

Opposite sides
of **dice**
always
add
up to **7.**

IT'S ILLEGAL
TO SELL A
HAUNTED
HOUSE
IN NEW YORK
WITHOUT
TELLING
THE BUYER.

Some elephant seals dive DEEPER than most submarines.

It gets so cold in Siberia that your breath can turn to ice in midair.

A BRITISH WEBSITE SELLS LAND ON MARS...

AND VENUS FOR £16.75 (ABOUT $29) AN ACRE.

A male ostrich can

roar like a **LION.**

Hippo sweat is red.

Some salamanders regrow their tails, legs, and even parts of their eyes.

A tiger's skin is  STRIPED like its fur.

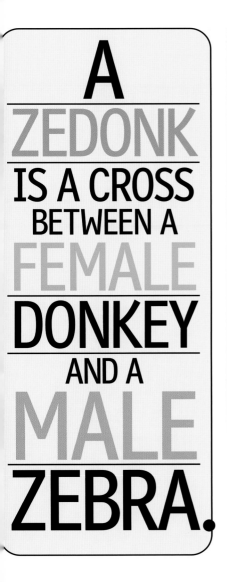

A ZEDONK IS A CROSS BETWEEN A FEMALE DONKEY AND A MALE ZEBRA.

Abracadabra used to be written in a triangle shape to keep away evil spirits.

ABRACADABRA
ABRACADABR
ABRACADAB
ABRACADA
ABRACAD
ABRACA
ABRAC
ABRA
ABR
AB
A

A Slinky can stretch from a sixth-floor window to the ground.

SOME ANTS MAKE THEMSELVES EXPLODE WHEN ATTACKED.

Chameleons change color in as fast as 20 seconds.

A **battery** can be made out of a **potato.**

JELLYFISH STING EVEN WHEN DEAD.

Your eyes move about 80 times a second.

A lobster's teeth are in its stomach.

A DOLPHIN CAN LEARN TO RECOGNIZE ITSELF IN THE MIRROR.

YOU CAN SEE AUTUMN LEAVES FROM SPACE.

There's a **heart-shaped coral reef** in Australia.

At least **12** rocks from **Mars** have landed on **Earth.**

A SLOTH WOULD TAKE A MONTH TO TRAVEL A SINGLE MILE.

A **U.S. dollar bill** can be folded in the same spot about **4,000 times** before it tears.

Chicks can **breathe** through their **shells.**

Pet hamsters **run** up to **eight miles** (13 km) **a night** on a **wheel.**

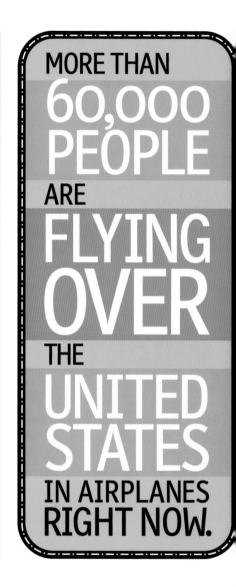

MORE THAN 60,000 PEOPLE ARE FLYING OVER THE UNITED STATES IN AIRPLANES RIGHT NOW.

New York

drifts about an inch (2.5 cm) farther from

London

every year.

In the open ocean, a **tsunami** sometimes travels as fast as a jet plane.

A mountain climber carried the Olympic torch to the top of Mount Everest.

Owls can't move their eyeballs.

ONE WAY

From Earth you always look at the **same side** of the **moon.**

THE BIGGEST BALD EAGLE NESTS WEIGH UP TO 4,000 POUNDS. (1,814 kg)

Kangaroos don't hop backward.

It's possible for people to get

goosebumps
on their faces.

Some **humming-birds** weigh less than a **penny.**

Tornadoes usually spin in opposite directions above and below the Equator.

It would take about **three years of nonstop pedaling** to bike to the moon.

as more than 200 feet.
(61 m)

Food passes **through the**

giant squid's

brain on the way to its stomach.

Clams can live to be more than a hundred years old.

WHO ARE YOU CALLING OLD?

The end of the minute hand on **London's Big Ben** clock travels about **118** miles (190 km) a year.

An avalanche can travel **80** MILES (129 km) AN HOUR.

In a lifetime, the average American drives approximately

627,000 miles (1,009,059 km)

or 25 times around the world— using enough gasoline to fill 3 fuel tankers.

A church IN THE Czech Republic HAS A chandelier made of human bones.

97%

of Earth's water
is saltwater.

Dust from Africa can travel all the way to Florida.

Humans can recognize about

10,000

different smells.

BUTTERFLIES taste food with their feet.

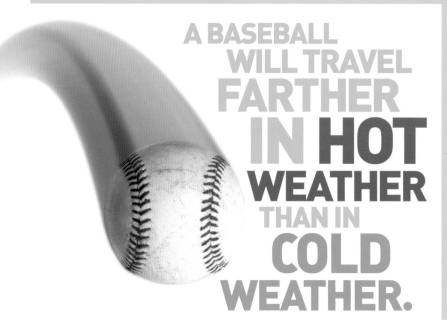

A BASEBALL WILL TRAVEL FARTHER **IN HOT** WEATHER THAN IN COLD WEATHER.

Snakes can't slither on glass.

A RESTAURANT OWNER MADE A **6,000-GALLON** (22,706 L) **MILKSHAKE**—ENOUGH TO FILL MORE THAN **100** BATHTUBS.

HIPPOS can be more dangerous than **LIONS.**

The fastest **falcon** can **outpace** a speeding **race car.**

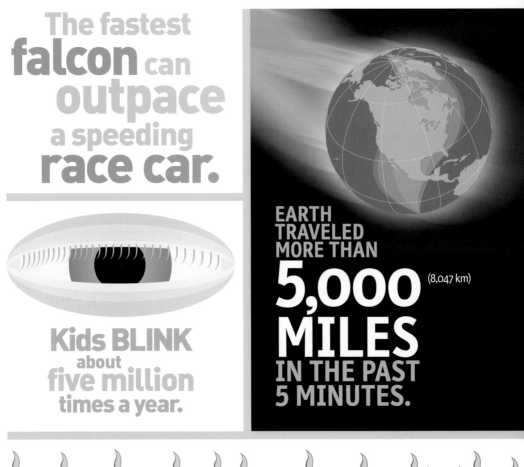

Kids BLINK about **five million** times a year.

EARTH
TRAVELED
MORE THAN

5,000 (8,047 km)
MILES

IN THE PAST
5 MINUTES.

(2,710 m)

Bakers in Turkey made an 8,891-foot-long cake—that's the length of about 114 tennis courts!

^^^^^^
The Himalayan **mountains** grow a half inch taller each year.

(1.3 cm)

.5

IF ABOUT
33 MILLION
PEOPLE
HELD HANDS,
THEY COULD MAKE
A CIRCLE AROUND
THE EQUATOR.

An ant can carry **50 TIMES** its body weight.

(That's like a kid carrying a car!)

In ancient Egypt, **mummies** **brains** were removed through the **nose.**

THE AVERAGE **$100** BILL CIRCULATES FOR **9** YEARS.

FOUR-THOUSAND-YEAR-OLD NOODLES WERE DISCOVERED IN ANCIENT RUINS IN CHINA.

A HUNDRED-YEAR-OLD CHOCOLATE BAR SOLD FOR NEARLY $700.

THE MOST EXPENSIVE ITEM EVER SOLD ON eBay WAS A $168-MILLION YACHT.

The planet **VENUS** spins backward.

IF YOU HEAT A DIAMOND TO 1405°F, (763°C) IT WILL TURN INTO VAPOR.

PEOPLE REPORT THE MOST UFO SIGHTINGS WHEN VENUS IS CLOSEST TO EARTH.

Australia was once a British prison colony.

The Asian vampire moth sometimes drinks the blood of animals

A New York man did a continuous series of somersaults for 12 miles, 390 yards. (357 m)

A person once **"hiccuped"** for **68** years.

A clock runs faster on a tall mountain than at sea level.

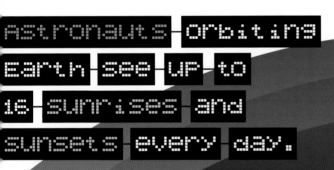

Astronauts orbiting Earth see up to 16 sunrises and sunsets every day.

Many birds' **feathers** weigh more than their **bones.**

A caterpillar has **more muscles** than a **human**.

You can fry an egg on a hot sidewa[lk]

ICELAND DOESN'T ONLY HAVE EARTHQUAKES; IT ALSO HAS ICEQUAKES.

...en it reaches 158°F. (70°C)

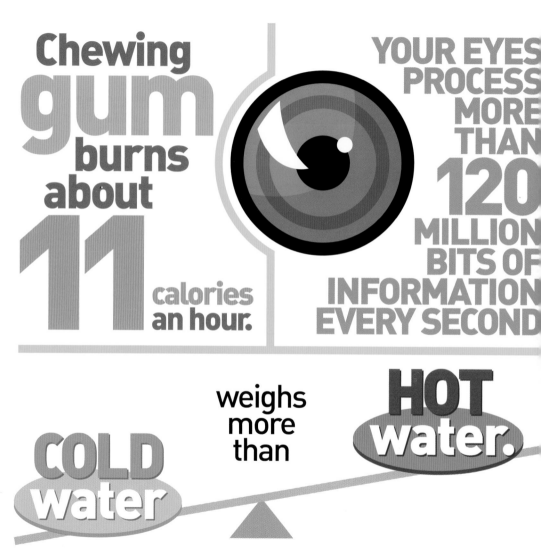

Chewing gum burns about **11** calories an hour.

YOUR EYES PROCESS MORE THAN **120** MILLION BITS OF INFORMATION EVERY SECOND

COLD water weighs more than **HOT water.**

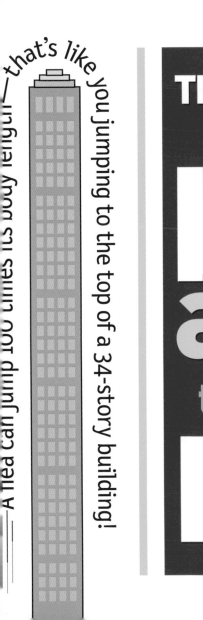

A flea can jump 100 times its body length—that's like you jumping to the top of a 34-story building!

The color red doesn't really make **bulls angry;** they are **●color-blind.**

No one knows what color dinosaurs were.

DAYS ARE LONGER THAN YEARS ON THE PLANET MERCURY.

THE FIRST CANDY CANES WERE MADE WITHOUT STRIPES.

Cat urine can glow under black light.

SOME FISH CHANGE FROM FEMALE TO MALE.

The average American eats enough **hamburger meat** in a lifetime to **equal the weight** of a family car.

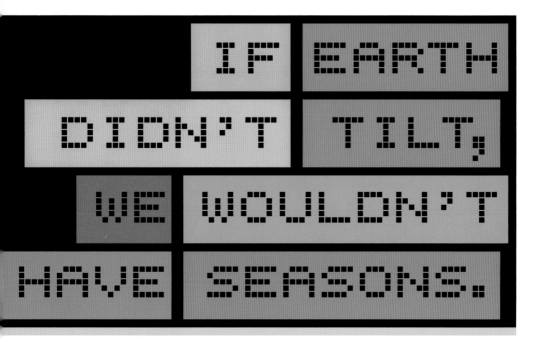

IF EARTH DIDN'T TILT, WE WOULDN'T HAVE SEASONS.

OUR PLANET HAS THE SAME AMOUNT OF **WATER TODAY** AS IT DID **100 MILLION** YEARS AGO.

A sea turtle

can weigh as much as a

water buffalo.

There are more **PLASTIC** **FLAMINGOS** IN THE U.S.A. **than** real ones.

VISION USES ONE-THIRD OF ALL YOUR BRAINPOWER.

PARACHUTES WERE INVENTED BEFORE AIRPLANES.

An electric eel produces a charge strong enough to

stun a horse.

Spiders have clear blood.

SOME RATS CAN SURVIVE WITHOUT WATER LONGER THAN CAMELS.

MORE PEOPLE LIVE IN CHINA TODAY THAN LIVED ON EARTH 150 YEARS AGO.

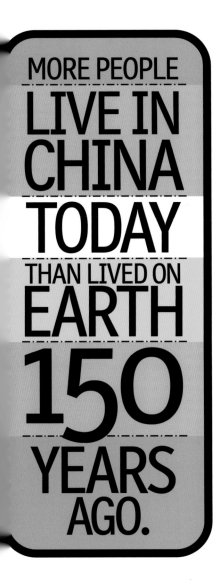

Ancient Egyptians believed that a person's **soul** was located in the **heart.**

Olympic gold medals are actually more than 90 percent **silver.**

119

The biggest gingerbread house was decorated with **4,750** pounds (2,155 kg) of icing—that's heavier than a **giraffe.**

IS THERE A RECORD FOR T CUTEST HOUSE

ASTRONAUTS' FOOTPRINTS STAY ON THE MOON FOREVER; THERE'S NO WIND TO BLOW THEM AWAY.

New Zealand HAS MORE sheep THAN people.

Giant TORTOISES KEEP GROWING FOR THEIR WHOLE LIVES.

MORE THAN
10 MILLION
MILLIONAIRES
ARE ALIVE
TODAY.

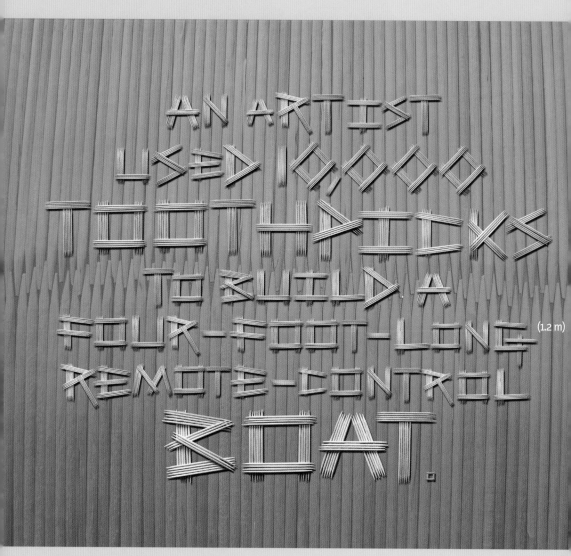

AN ARTIST USED 1,000,000 TOOTHPICKS TO BUILD A FOUR-FOOT-LONG (1.2 m) REMOTE-CONTROL BOAT.

EARTHWORMS HAVE 5 HEARTS.

Ladybugs squirt smelly liquid from their knees when they get scared.

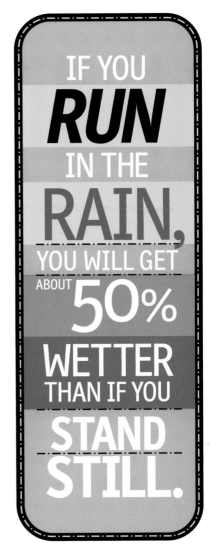

IF YOU **RUN** IN THE RAIN, YOU WILL GET ABOUT 50% WETTER THAN IF YOU STAND STILL.

IN SOME
PLACES THERE ARE
ABOUT AS MANY
INSECTS
IN ONE SQUARE MILE (2.6 sq km)
AS THERE ARE PEOPLE
ON THE ENTIRE
PLANET.

HONEYBEES CAN BE TRAINED TO DETECT EXPLOSIVES.

Traffic lights were invented

before : CARS.

THERE ARE MORE STARS IN THE UNIVERSE THAN GRAINS OF SAND ON EARTH.

THE LONGEST MONOPOLY GAME PLAYED IN A BATHTUB LASTED **99** HOURS.

Blue whales ARE THE **largest animals** THAT EVER **lived—** THEY'RE EVEN BIGGER THAN **dinosaurs!**

CLEOPATRA BECAME THE QUEEN OF EGYPT WHEN SHE WAS ONLY A TEENAGER.

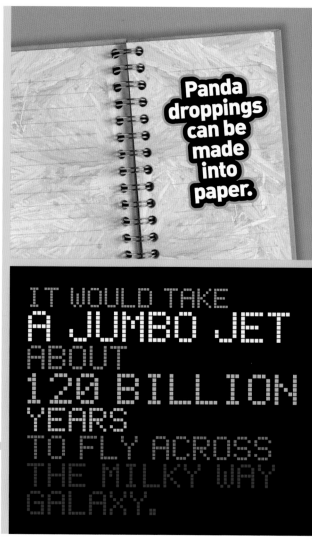

Panda droppings can be made into paper.

IT WOULD TAKE A JUMBO JET ABOUT 120 BILLION YEARS TO FLY ACROSS THE MILKY WAY GALAXY.

The largest dinosaurs were vegetarians.

A
pet
goldfish
in England
lived
to be
43
years old.

RED
RAIN
HAS
FALLEN
IN PARTS
OF EUROPE
AND ASIA.

Catnip can affect lions and tigers.

A 300-YEAR-OLD HURRICANE ON JUPITER IS STILL GOING STRONG!

THE WORLD'S HEAVIEST ONION WEIGHED MORE THAN A MAN'S HEAD.

In **Peru** it's considered **good luck** to wear yellow **underwear** on New Year's **Day.**

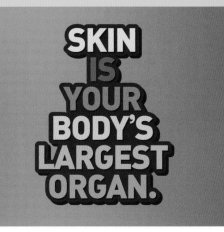

SKIN IS YOUR BODY'S LARGEST ORGAN.

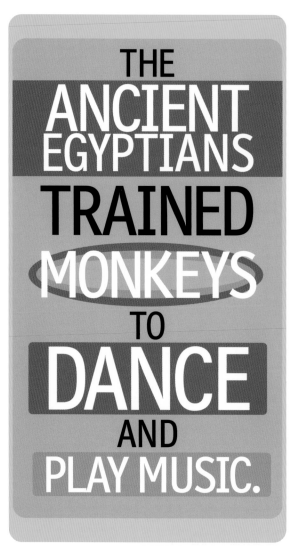

THE ANCIENT EGYPTIANS TRAINED MONKEYS TO DANCE AND PLAY MUSIC.

Mike the **chicken** lived for **18 months** without **a head,** from **1945** to **1947.**

A Harley-Davidson MOTORCYCLE WAS designed to look like a giant hamburger.

Chimpanzees, monkeys, dogs, mice, and a guinea pig have all journeyed into space.

One of the largest man-made islands is shaped like a palm tree.

You can buy a **diamond dog collar** for about **$3 million.**

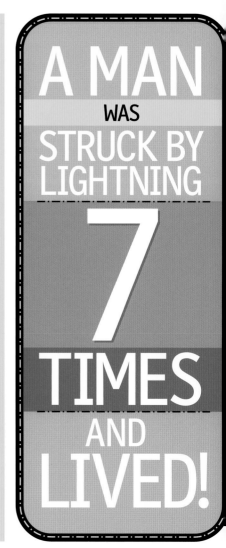

A MAN WAS STRUCK BY LIGHTNING 7 TIMES AND LIVED!

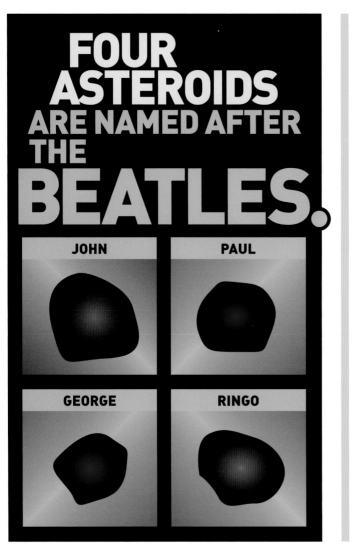

FOUR ASTEROIDS ARE NAMED AFTER THE BEATLES.

| JOHN | PAUL |
| GEORGE | RINGO |

If you fell into a black hole, you'd stretch out like s p a g h e t t i.

Crickets detect sound through their knees.

THERE IS CELL PHONE RECEPTION AT THE SUMMIT OF MOUNT EVEREST.

SOME **wild** turkeys **run** UP TO **25** miles (40 km) **an hour.**

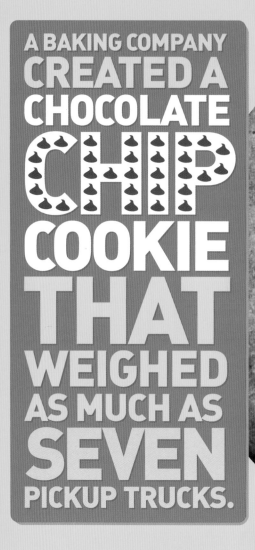

A BAKING COMPANY
CREATED A
CHOCOLATE
CHIP
COOKIE
THAT
WEIGHED
AS MUCH AS
SEVEN
PICKUP TRUCKS.

A COMET is a gigantic ball of dirt and ice.

The **smallest** monkey is about as tall as a **toothbrush.**

A GRIZZLY BEAR CAN RUN AS FAST AS A HORSE.

Astronauts have grown potatoes on the space shuttle.

A man 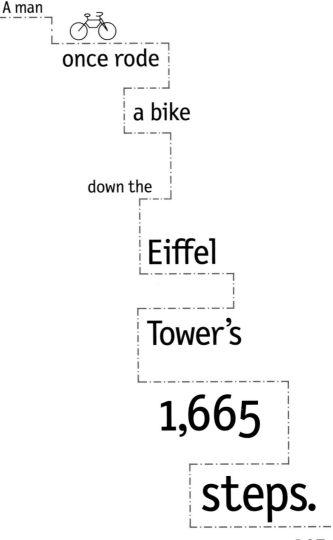 once rode a bike down the Eiffel Tower's 1,665 steps.

The holes in **Swiss cheese** are called "eyes."

A
CANADIAN
COMPANY
BOTTLES
WATER
THAT COMES FROM
12,000-
TO
15,000-
YEAR-OLD
ICEBERGS.

A HIGHWAY RUNS THROUGH THE MIDDLE OF AN OFFICE BUILDING IN OSAKA, JAPAN.

THE WORLD'S MOST EXPENSIVE TREE HOUSE, LOCATED IN THE UNITED KINGDOM, COST £3.7 MILLION TO BUILD.

(about $6.1 million)

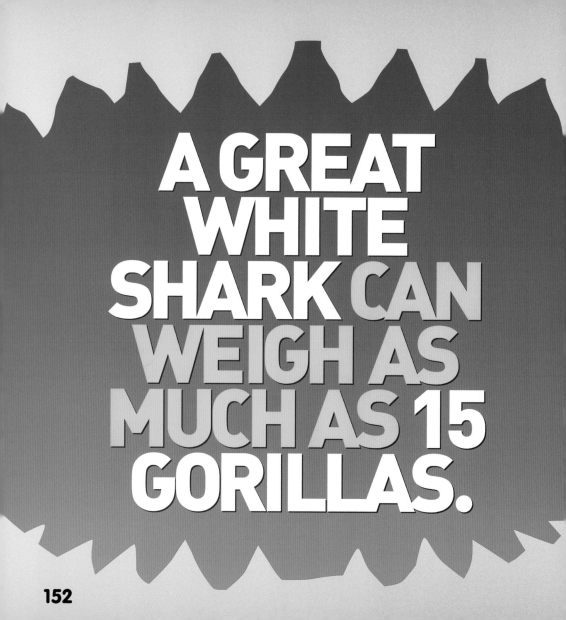

A GREAT WHITE SHARK CAN WEIGH AS MUCH AS 15 GORILLAS.

THE
WORLD'S
SMALLEST
FROG
IS THE SIZE OF A
CHEERIO.

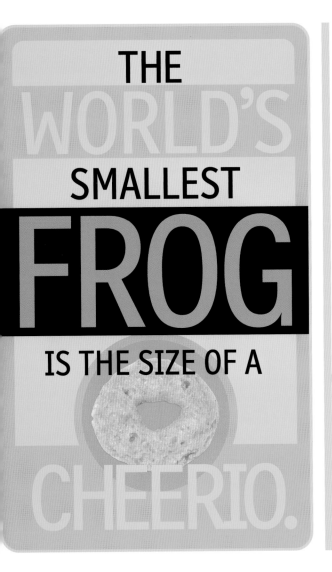

A pizza topped with 24-karat gold sold for more than $4,000.

The world's **termites outweigh** the world's **people.**

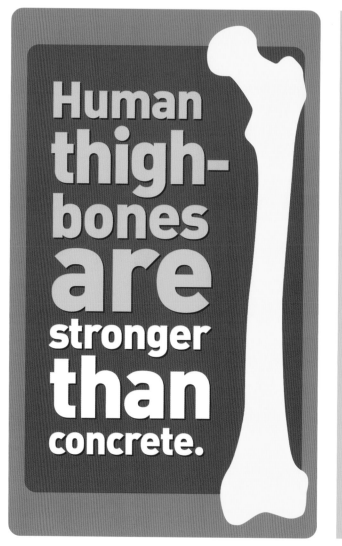

Human thigh-bones are stronger than concrete.

THE PLANET **EARTH** ROTATES **1.5** MILLISECONDS **SLOWER** EVERY CENTURY.

Snowflakes get smaller **as the** TEMPERATURE **DROPS.**

A JELLYFISH CAN BE AS SMALL AS A THIMBLE OR AS LARGE AS TWO WASHING MACHINES.

A STACK OF A BILLION DOLLAR BILLS WEIGHS MORE THAN 15 ARMY TANKS.

A **newborn kangaroo** is about as long as a **paper clip.**

Giant anteaters c

A BABY PORCUPINE IS CALLED A PORCUPETTE.

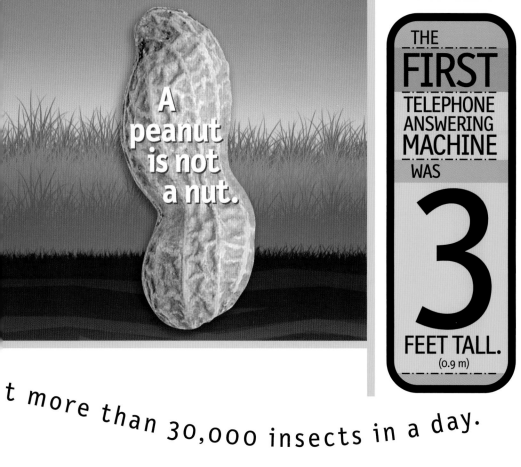

A peanut is not a nut.

THE **FIRST** TELEPHONE ANSWERING **MACHINE** WAS **3** FEET TALL. (0.9 m)

t more than 30,000 insects in a day.

There are
31,556,926
seconds
in a year.

THE
BIGGEST
INHABITED
PALACE
ON
EARTH

(IN THE SOUTHEAST ASIAN COUNTRY OF BRUNEI)

HAS

1,788
ROOMS.

A CLOUD CAN WEIGH MORE THAN A MILLION POUNDS.
(453,593 kg)

The Amazon rain forest is home to giant rodents— called capybaras— that are about as tall as German shepherds.

The Chihuahua is the world's smallest dog breed.

Most experts believe that **birds** are descended from **dinosaurs.**

MARSHMALLOWS WERE ORIGINALLY MADE FROM ROOTS OF A PLANT CALLED THE MARSH-MALLOW.

20% of the food we eat is used to **fuel THE BRAIN.**

EVERY DAY IS ABOUT 55 BILLIONTHS OF A SECOND LONGER THAN THE DAY BEFORE IT.

The skin of a golden poison dart frog contains enough toxins to kill up to **100 people.**

Gorillas  **burp** when they're happy.

HUMMINGBIRDS are the only birds that can fly BACKWARD.

ABOUT ONE-QUARTER OF THE

body's bones are
in the feet —that's 52 out of more than 200!

A SPACE SUIT WEIGHS 280 POUNDS— (127 kg) WITHOUT AN ASTRONAUT IN IT.

Elephants sometimes make purr-like sounds when content.

Baby RATTLESNAKES are born without RATTLES.

The Milky Way is made up of **some 100 billion stars.**

SOME SAND DUNES *BARK.*

You use 72 different muscles every time you talk.

Your body contains about
60,000
miles
(96,561 km)
of blood
vessels.

Strawberries have more VITAMIN C than oranges.

Palm trees grew at the North Pole about 55 million years ago.

A SNAIL WOULD TAKE ABOUT **220 HOURS TO CRAWL ONE MILE** (1.6 km)

NONSTOP.

The **Basenji,** a dog from **Africa,** yodels instead of **barking.**

ON NEPTUNE THE WIND BLOWS UP TO 1,243 MILES (2,000 km) AN HOUR.

"HAPPY BIRTHDAY" WAS THE FIRST SONG TRANSMITTED FROM SPACE TO EARTH.

THE WORLD'S LONGEST
mountain range
is under the
sea.

An average adult's
skin
weighs about 11
pounds.
(5 kg)

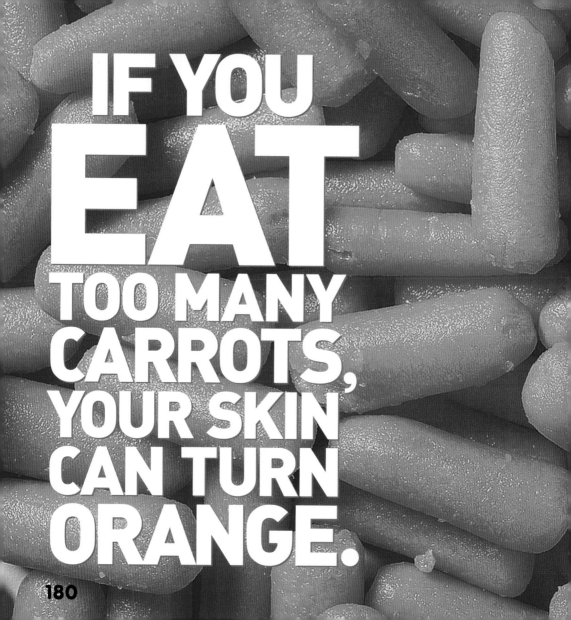

IF YOU EAT TOO MANY CARROTS, YOUR SKIN CAN TURN ORANGE.

A CROCODILE CAN'T STICK ITS TONGUE OUT.

THE NUMBER OF TIMES **some crickets chirp** each second **can be used to estimate** the **temperature.**

You lose about **NINE POUNDS** (4.1 kg) of skin cells every year.

You can't move your body when you're dreaming.

The
face in the
"Mona Lisa"
has no
eye-
brOws.

You're almost a **half inch** taller (1.3 cm) in the morning than in the evening.

Astronauts can't whistle ON THE MOON.

Death Valley, California, IS THE hottest PLACE IN North America.

Human ears evolved from ancient **FISH GILLS.**

THAT'S WEIRD!

THE LONGEST RECORDED
FLIGHT OF A

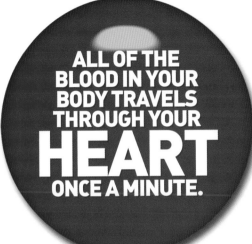

ALL OF THE BLOOD IN YOUR BODY TRAVELS THROUGH YOUR HEART ONCE A MINUTE.

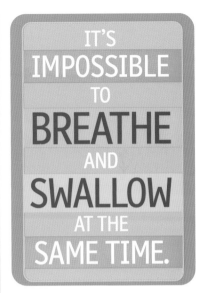

IT'S IMPOSSIBLE TO BREATHE AND SWALLOW AT THE SAME TIME.

CHICKEN IS 13 SECONDS.

THE OLDEST HUMAN FOOTPRINT EVER FOUND IS 350,000 YEARS OLD.

A 100-POUND PERSON (45 kg) WOULD WEIGH 38 POUNDS (17 kg) ON MARS.

Your hair grows faster IN WARM WEATHER.

THE MALE KILLER WHALE'S DORSAL (BACK) FIN IS ALMOST SIX FEET (1.8 m) HIGH— THE HEIGHT OF A TALL MAN.

A **LIZARD-LIKE** REPTILE CALLED A TUATARA HAS A **THIRD EYE** ON TOP OF ITS **HEAD.**

THE YEAR
2020
is the next time you can see a full moon on Halloween.

GHOST BATS are some of the only bats with WHITE FUR.

Sharks have **eight** senses.

A **coyote** can hear a mouse moving **under** a foot of snow.

Humans have only five.

The **human** **body** contains enough **iron** to make a two-inch **nail.**

(5.1 cm)

CROCODILES HAVE BEEN AROUND FOR ABOUT **200** **MILLION YEARS.**

MOUNTAIN LIONS CAN WHISTLE.

THE **LEANING TOWER** OF **PISA** **STARTED TILTING BEFORE** THE **BUILDING** WAS COMPLETED.

It's impossible for a person to **sink** in the **Dead Sea.**

Your heart is about the same size as your **fist.**

THE HORNED DINOSAUR DRACOREX HOGWARTSIA WAS NAMED AFTER **HOGWARTS,** HARRY POTTER'S SCHOOL.

MORE WATER IS IN THE PACIFIC OCEAN THAN IN ALL OF THE OTHER SEAS AND OCEANS COMBINED.

99%

of people can't
lick their
elbows.

(But 90% of people who read this will try!)

FACTFINDER

Illustrations are indicated
by **boldface.**

200

Since 1888, the National Geographic Society has funded more than 12,000 research, exploration, and preservation projects around the world. The Society receives funds from National Geographic Partners, LLC, funded in part by your purchase. A portion of the proceeds from this book supports this vital work. To learn more, visit www.natgeo.com/info.

For more information, visit www.nationalgeographic.com, call 1-800-647-5463, or write to the following address:
National Geographic Partners, LLC
1145 17th Street NW
Washington, D.C. 20036-4688 U.S.A.

Staff for This Book

Robin Terry, *Project Editor*
Eva Absher, *Art Direction and Design*
Lori Renda, Jay Sumner, *Illustrations Editors*
Sharon Thompson, Kelsey Turek, *Research*
Grace Hill, *Associate Managing Editor*
Jeff Reynolds, *Marketing Director, Children's Books*
Lewis R. Bassford, *Production Manager*
Susan Borke, *Legal and Business Affairs*

Based on the "Weird But True" department in NATIONAL GEOGRAPHIC KIDS magazine

Jonathan Halling, *Design Director*
Robin Terry, *Senior Editor*
Kelley Miller, *Photo Editor*
Sharon Thompson, *Writer-Researcher*
Marilyn Terrell, Mridula Srinivasan, Jeffrey Wandel, *Freelance Researchers*

Manufacturing and Quality Management

Christopher A. Liedel, *Chief Financial Officer*
Phillip L. Schlosser, *Vice President*
Chris Brown, *Technical Director*
Rachel Faulise, *Manufacturing Manager*
Nicole Elliott, *Manufacturing Manager*

Visit us online:
Kids: nationalgeographic.com/kids
Parents: nationalgeographic.com
Teachers: nationalgeographic.com/education
Librarians: ngchildrensbooks.org

For information about special discounts for bulk purchases, please contact National Geographic Books Special Sales: ngspecsales@ngs.org

For rights or permissions inquiries, please contact National Geographic Books Subsidiary Rights: ngbookrights@ngs.org

NATIONAL GEOGRAPHIC and Yellow Border Design are trademarks of the National Geographic Society, used under license.

Library of Congress Cataloging-in-Publication Data
Weird but true: 300 outrageous facts.
    p. cm.
Includes index.
ISBN 978-1-4263-0594-8 (pbk. : alk. paper)
1. Curiosities and wonders--Juvenile literature.
I. National Geographic Society (U.S.)
AG243.W39 2010 001.9--dc22
2009028459

Printed in China
16/PPS/4-BX

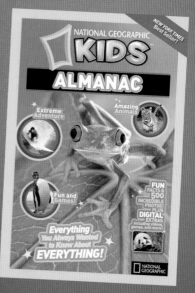